Across the Jordan

Being an explanation
of insights received,
towards a better
understanding of the
Christian experience,
with additional
resources provided.

RONALD E. BAKKER

ISBN 978-1-257-87753-9

Links to purchase or download updated or revised editions may be available over time at:
www.AcrossTheJordan.com

Comments, questions and requests can be made online at:
www.AcrossTheJordan.com

rev.5p 7-26-11

TABLE OF CONTENTS

The Dilemma

When I became a Christian, I understood Christianity in these basic terms: I was lost, but now I am saved. We can illustrate the idea of these two stages. In the left stage we might use words like sinner, worldly, heathen, unsaved, or lost to describe the inhabitants. In the stage on the right we might use words like born again, saved, converted, or saint. The area between the two stages, we will call a transition point, and we might label it "conversion, rebirth, accepting Christ" etc. As a Christian I had crossed over from one side to the other.

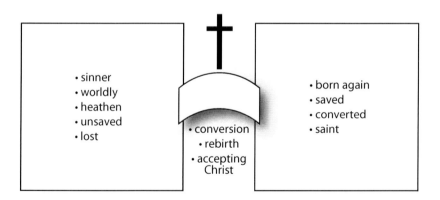

These two stages were largely the sum of how I understood everything around me. Later on, I mentally amended the stage to the right and lengthened it because I saw Christianity as being progressive... advancing. Christians called this Sanctification - the process of Christianity. And there were lots of things to attain in this process - many big things were promised like perfected love, perfect peace, Christ-likeness, and victory over sins.

But it was these big things that caused me problems. You see, I wasn't attaining them, or even getting close to them. Andrew Murray once wrote "*the blessings of the higher Christian life were often like the objects exposed in a shop window,--one could see them clearly and yet could not reach them. If told to stretch out his hand and take, a man would answer, I cannot; there is a thick pane of plate-glass between me and them. And even so Christians may see clearly the blessed promises of perfect peace and rest, of overflowing love and joy, of abiding communion and fruitfulness, and yet feel that there was something between them, hindering the true possession.*" What was the thick pane of glass? What was it that was hindering us from reaching these most precious promises?

Because I was unable to lay hold of these "blessings of the higher Christian life", my life became more and more about being "nice" rather than being truly good. I tried hard to appear to be a good Christian - smiling, gentle, careful, and kind. I prayed daily that God would make me good, that He would change my nature, but it only became worse. Over time I was disillusioned by this life of pretense, a facade of kindness was not what I had signed up for. God had called me with power, and in the beginning His spirit was unmistakable in my life, and now after some years, was my life to be a pantomime of polite words and smiles hiding the awful burden of sin hidden inside me? No. I would rather be an honest sinner than a dishonest Christian.

Then for over twenty years I wrestled with the same questions, God pushing me to move forward, never letting me go, and me struggling, studying and praying. What was the answer? I read the gospels and the book of Acts and saw these empowered Christians having a close personal walk with Christ, possessing the great gifts that Christ promised, and having a powerful influence on those around them. This was not mere kindness, but an explosive exhibition of the Spirit's power displayed - healing the sick, casting out demons and delivering the gospel with power. Were not these men the same as us? Possessors of the same promises? Did God hinder us from receiving these gifts? Or in fact, did we hinder God?

I wanted the fullness of the Spirit in my life, but struggled daily with the same sins, the same weakness, the same self.

Let us look at the two stages again. Here I was, in the stage on the right... and yet I had no peace, I often hated my brothers, felt no real pity for the unsaved, fought constantly with sin and fell regularly. Was I then, in fact, on the stage on the left? No, I had chosen Christ, been profoundly called by Him. His law and His voice were ever before me. My soul longed to be healed, I begged for victory, and I desired the good things He offered,

But I was ever hindered by that "thick pane of glass".

So I began to question my fellow travelers. And I discovered that same malaise existed in their own lives. In general, I found two camps:

1. Those who, like myself, had not obtained the fullness of the promises, but desired them still, and strove daily to draw closer to God to receive them and

2. Those who had learned through repetitive failure that obtaining the gifts seemed impossible and who had restructured their concept of Christianity so that it no longer made such demands upon them. They in fact changed either their theology so that they were found acceptable in God's eyes, or they pushed the receipt of the promises into some future time before Christ's coming so that they were no longer threatened by the absence of power in their lives.

The result though seemed the same. Group #1 was tormented and virtually powerless, and Group #2 was satisfied and virtually powerless. And the result? A church body that was also virtually powerless.

What was the answer?

Maybe we were all in fact, not in the stage on the right at all. Maybe we were all on the left... and had deceived ourselves into thinking we were on the right.

Maybe we were on the right but each time we sinned or failed, we bounced back over to the left... and had to ask forgiveness to get back to the right.

Maybe a life of constant sin and resultant guilt was indeed all there was to Christianity, and He would fix it all just before we died or just before the second coming.

Maybe I should try harder.
Maybe I was just impatient?
Maybe I was one of the opiated masses.
Maybe I should pray harder, longer.

Maybe I should read the bible more. Maybe I should get rid of my movie collection, maybe I should stop watching TV, maybe I should volunteer at a soup kitchen. Maybe I should repay everything I stole, ask forgiveness of everyone I injured, and fast for a week.

And all these things I tried, and kneeled in my closet, stood in empty parking lots at midnight, and wandered alone in the woods, and cried out to God..."What is the answer?" And when He answered, or rather, when I was able to hear Him, He said

"There are three stages, not two"

THREE STAGES

"There are three stages, not two" The very idea stopped me in my tracks, I looked again at everything I knew and had to start evaluating everything from the beginning.

What even would a third stage mean?

1. If there is a third stage, then it must mean, by inference, that we are to journey on towards it. Immediately it makes the second stage a place of transition.
2. If the second stage is transitional, then it is no wonder that we found it so uncomfortable living there.
3. If the second stage is transitional then there must be an identifiable system to transition out of it, in a similar way to the way we transitioned into it.
4. If there is a third stage, then those of us who believed in the two stage principal must have *mis-assigned some of the biblical terms we used to describe the second stage* - some of those terms must apply to the third stage.
5. There must be a real purpose to the existence of the third stage... God created this place to be occupied.

So lets add the third stage and the two transitional bridges between the stages, to our diagram (next page). This will function as the visual reference as we proceed to look at the evidence. It will also help us later to update the labels of each stage, and the transitions between them.

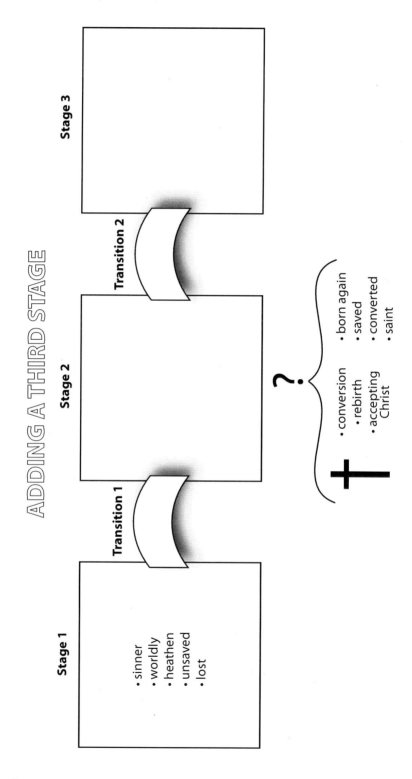

ADDING A THIRD STAGE

Stage 1
- sinner
- worldly
- heathen
- unsaved
- lost

Transition 1

Stage 2

Transition 2

Stage 3

?

+

- conversion
- rebirth
- accepting Christ
- born again
- saved
- converted
- saint

We can see now the second stage as a place to journey through rather than to reside in. Our real goal was the third stage. But now we have all the important transition labels like "conversion" and "rebirth" unassigned because there are two transitional points in which to assign them. What goes where, and indeed what are the latter two stages?

The Lord initially showed me two references to help identify the stages, these were
1. A metaphor in an Old Testament event,
2. A dream from Ellen White.

Let's look at these references briefly, and then we'll look at each stage and transition in detail.

1. The Old Testament's grandest metaphor... the Exodus.

The Israelites were slaves for over 400 years before Moses. They had no power, no authority, no freedom of worship. They were in bondage - a biblical metaphor for our sin captivity. There are three clearly defined areas on the Israelites journey to the Promised Land, and two clearly defined transitions. If the Exodus serves as a living metaphor of the Christian life as Paul suggests it does (I Cor 10, Heb 3,4), then this is a powerful argument for the third stage.

2. In 1868, Ellen White had a dream that she recorded as "An Impressive Dream". In that dream she saw a group of people ascending a long path that terminated at a deep chasm, and with the help of divine cords they swing across the chasm into a "beautiful field". Here again we see three sharply defined stages, and two transition points. (The *Impressive Dream* can be read in Appendix 1 - Page 33)

Now using these metaphors, let's look again at our three stages and two transitions.

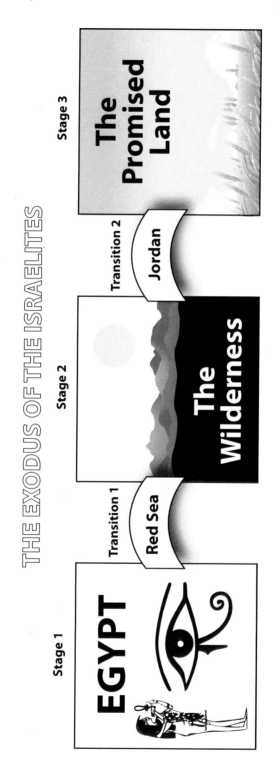

THE EXODUS OF THE ISRAELITES

Stage 1 — EGYPT

Transition 1 — Red Sea

Stage 2 — The Wilderness

Transition 2 — Jordan

Stage 3 — The Promised Land

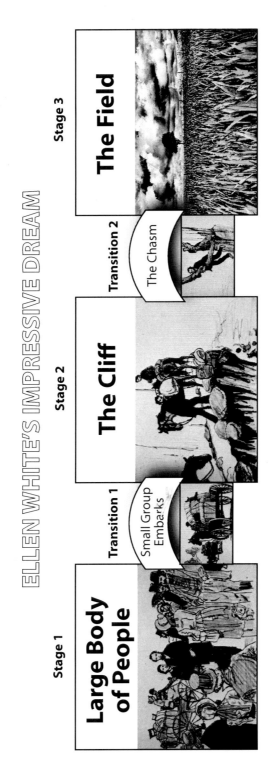

Across the Jordan

Stage 1: In Slavery to Sin

In the Exodus metaphor, Egypt is the land of bondage, and it gives us the clearest indication of what it means to be in stage one. We are without choice or control over our own actions. Day by day the children of Israel worked and lived for the Pharaoh. Any freedom of choice they had was illusional beneath the oppressive structure of their bondage. Day by day they were in total submission to another master. They built temples to Pharaoh's grandeur, roads for his chariots, and buildings to house his gods.

They might choose to be nice, but they were still slaves. They might help their neighbours, but they were still slaves. The only choice that would significantly change their lives - to no longer be a slave, was beyond their control and ability. Slaves they were, and would remain without active intervention.

This is the life of slavery we were born into when mankind separated from God in Eden. Each of us is born separated and distant from God, and a gulf stands between Himself and us. In time the former Children of God worshipped the graven images of their masters, lived the same lives of debauchery, and no longer knew their Lord.

Egypt is where we all begin. John says of us that "*all have sinned, and come short of the glory of God*". There is no one that does not require the active redemptive work of God. There is no one born without the disconnection. "*If we say that we have no sin, we deceive ourselves, and the truth is not in us.*" We are all metaphorically slaves in Egypt.

Across the Jordan

Everything we build in Egypt is without purpose, or only serves the greater purposes of our slave-master.

Every decision you make in that life is a decision that must be approved of by your master and must inevitably serve his ends. What you believe is serving self, actually serves another. All you are, all you think you possess, all apparent status, are corrupt illusions. All end in death. *"Do you not know that when you present yourselves to someone as slaves for obedience, you are slaves of the one whom you obey, either of sin resulting in death, or of obedience resulting in righteousness?" Rom:6:16*

Transition 1: The Red Sea

God's people were captives in Egypt. But with great miracles, God not only cowed the Egyptian prince into submission, but markedly displayed his power to His own people. For the first time in their lives they began to understand that their God was a God of power and substance. Moses was sent to call them, and they responded by following.

As they fled Egypt, they encountered the first barrier. The Red Sea. Moses was told to raise his staff against the waters and when he did so the waters of the Red Sea parted, and the people walked through the Sea as upon dry ground. There is no natural way of escape - no system you can follow, no way out of Egypt except as God makes one. Unless God made the way, they would all be slaves yet. *"Jesus saith unto him, I am the way, the truth, and the life: no man cometh unto the Father, but by me."*

And without the sacrifice of Christ, the entire world would be in the same predicament. God would still long to save them, they might long to be saved, but the gulf that was created by Adam's sin would be too great to be crossed without extraordinary intervention. God could not simply carry them across that gulf without ignoring His own law - the principles upon which the universe were built. Nor could He save them while they lived as slaves to another master. But Christ, coming in the flesh, bridged that gulf, so that *"that he (God) might be just, and the justifier of him which believeth in Jesus."* God could now both keep His law, and rescue mankind from their predicament.

This is the means by which we enter into the initial relationship

Across the Jordan

with God. God calls us from the place of sin to cross over into a relationship with Him.

"God is faithful, by whom ye were called unto the fellowship of his Son Jesus Christ our Lord."

"But God commendeth his love toward us, in that, while we were yet sinners, Christ died for us."

This is the first transition, God calls us, and we respond. He makes a way through the Red Sea. We cross over the bridge that is the Christ, for He is the Way. This is the first profound discovery of God and changes the purpose, direction, and passions of the believer.

So profound is this first experience that we can be forgiven thinking that it is the culmination of God's plan. To leave Egypt and cross the Red Sea! The miracles wrought! The power displayed! And who but God could have done it? And so we speak of the day we were saved from sin and slavery, and mark it with a baptism, like the Jews themselves holding the great Passover Feast.

And it is right to esteem God for this day, for the building of this bridge emptied heaven of its greatest resource, the angels are in awe of it, and the very heart of God is revealed in it.

But the journey is not over yet, there are yet paths to trod, and there are more miracles yet.

Stage 2: The Wilderness

For over four hundred years the children of promise had dwelled in darkness. What they knew of God was only imperfectly remembered. And with a rush of power, God was once more in their lives. Moses came to rescue them, and they hardly even understood what that might mean. The plagues reigned down upon their enemies. They gained status, fear, and respect in the eyes of their captors. Their God was doing this. And that last terrible night that they had spent in Egypt with mothers and fathers weeping and screaming for their dead, the children of Israel huddled in their homes, unsure how a little blood on the door post could save them. Then in the morning they left, all in a rush, carrying their unmade bread upon their backs, pillaging the wealth of a nation, they looked at each other and could hardly believe what was happening.

Who was this man Moses, who was this God?.

They were afraid, and reticent at the shores of the Red Sea - they were not even sure they wanted to be here *"Is not this the word that we did tell thee in Egypt, saying, Let us alone, that we may serve the Egyptians? For it had been better for us to serve the Egyptians, than that we should die in the wilderness."* And then, later that same day, to be ushered across the vastness of the sea upon dry ground, their hearts melting in them for fear, but Moses leading them forward and the pillar of fire following behind, they crossed.

On the morning of the next day they awoke in a new land. Everything that had defined them for the last half millennia was now no longer relevant. They were no longer slaves, but what were they? The trades they had performed under Pharaoh were now of little use. They had no skills for this new land. What was needed was food and water and there seemed no simple method of acquiring either in this wasteland. And even the servitude that they did know - that the Egyptians taught them - was worthless to God because it was a servitude born of oppression and fear, one that only resulted in grumbling and reluctant obedience.

They were a people without context, without definition, and they stood on the shore of a discarded and desolate land with a God they neither knew nor understood.

But it was not God's will that they live here. It was never God's will that his people live among the sand and the rocks. His great promise to Abraham spoken over 430 years previously was not that his people would be like the stars of the sky and that they would possess a barren land and suffer at the hands of the elements. No! The great promise of God was that they would occupy a new land, a land flowing with milk and honey. So what were they doing here? Did not they ask the same question? *"Would to God we had died by the hand of the LORD in the land of Egypt, when we sat by the flesh pots, and when we did eat bread to the full; for ye have brought us forth into this wilderness, to kill this whole assembly with hunger."* (Exodus 16:3)

It is imperative that we understand that God never purposed his children to occupy the wilderness for any extended period of time. They were to journey through it until they arrived at the promised land. And that is the path upon which Moses took them. It was only their subsequent refusal to enter that land that cursed an entire generation of Israelites to wander in the desert for 40 years.

God wants us too, to move through this land, not to dwell here, not to build houses here or to raise our children here. God wants us to go up and possess a new land, the land of promise. But first we must pass through the wilderness, and Ellen White's "Impressive Dream" might help us to understand why.

Ellen White's dream opens at the foot of a mountain path. There was a large group gathered there but only a portion set off up the mountain. This is the first transition. Now it is important to note the progress of the little band as they move up the cliff face, for it is a powerful image.

Step by step the narrowing path forces the group to shed themselves of the wagons, horses and luggage that they began the journey with. Eventually the ledge becomes so narrow that the group has to remove even their shoes and socks in order to stay the path. As the group loses more and more of their dependence on the narrowing ledge, ropes are let down to help them maintain balance. As the ledge narrows even more, the ropes get thicker to give them greater and greater support.

This is the reason for the second stage. For it is here that we are separated from anything that creates in us a dependence that is not upon God - anything. Though we might agree that the travelers up the mountain might need to lose their dependence on their loaded wagons, who would deny them their shoes or socks on such a journey? God's requirement is simple - it all must go. This is not simply about ownership, or physical things, this goes far beyond the possession of goods. God requires that every hidden trust in yourself or others, every hope founded in your own ability, intelligence, or nobility is discarded in this land. Here it is left and here it must stay. All self must die in the wilderness.

And such a routing for every vestige of self in the soul is painful. Look to those who journey up the cliff. There is the blood of those who have gone before, there are the fearful cries, there is the hesitant step. This is no easy land to inhabit, for it is here that God scourges the soul of every crutch that has supported it in the past. Trial upon trial reveal our weakness, and each weakness is an opportunity to turn to God. Whether your dependence is upon money, an impressive theological vocabulary, or the commendations of world, all will be stripped of you should you adhere to the path. Did we think we might escape it? Did we think that there was a way up the path through mental assent, or well read understanding, or lengthy prayers? There is no short path. And there is no entrance to the third stage except as we travel this hard road.

For the Israelites, it was the wilderness that was to teach them. When they first reached the borders of the promised land, they were not yet fully instructed, they would not enter in. *"We be not able to go up against the people; for they [are] stronger than we."* *"there we saw the giants"* (Numbers 13:31/33). Despite the miracles that God had shown them, they had learned to depend only on themselves - and they feared the promised land more than they feared the wrath of God. So they wandered, and day by day they hungered, day by day their efforts to bring forth food from the ground were thwarted. Of themselves they could produce nothing. And day by day for forty years the manna fell. This was their strong cord, their hold from above. The rocks gave water, the sky gave food, and of themselves they could do nothing. This was the daily message of the wilderness. Depend on God. Humble yourselves before the Lord. You can do nothing.

And when they again met the opportunity to enter in, they bowed their heads and let God lead. They were fearful, but trusting. *"God holds the cord. We need not fear."* but still when Ellen White gripped that cord, and placed all her weight upon it, *"The sweat was dropping from my face, and I felt such anguish as I had never felt before."* This is the fire by which men's souls are tried. And, again, there is no route but this one, no path by which you can attain the promised land, except by this path. *"A fearful struggle was before us. Should we fail here, all the difficulties of our journey had been experienced for nought."* she wrote.

But it was God who searched you out in Egypt, God who placed your feet on the beginning of this path, God who parted the sea, God who taught you what was required at Sinai, and God who sustained you when you realized that you couldn't accomplish it. And God would not leave you now. *"He will not fail us now. He has brought us thus far in safety."*

The ropes from above *"had increased in size until they were as large as our bodies."* What a wonderful God. A thin cord could have supported our whole weight here, for it was a cord made by the hand of God. But we saw it as such a size and strength that we could be persuaded to trust it, to put all our weight upon it and finally lift our feet from the cliff's edge.

Whatever this journey represents, it represents the utter separation from dependence on self, for in this one sin lies all others. Our self-dependence, self-reliance, self-respect, are all aspects of the same sin that cast Satan from heaven and testifies to the gulf that exists between God and ourselves. No amount of dependence upon self is acceptable to God nor should be acceptable to us.

You cannot have one foot on the cliff, and one in the green field. The chasm is too wide. And so in Sinai, as on the journey up the path, day by the day the lesson was one that we must depend upon God. Abandon the hope we have yet in ourselves to do anything. For what is born of self is nothing but self. You can build no holy temple on rotten pillars. We may satisfy self as completely with theology and the prayerful observances as we satisfied it with the pursuits of the world in our previous life, for did not the Pharisees do as much?

But this temple, this self, this pretense to righteousness must all be abandoned in this place, it is the point and purpose of this place. And we are just travelers here. This task must be completed. Self must die in this wilderness that the new life might be born in us across the Jordan.

Across the Jordan

Transition 2: The Jordan

They now knew in their hearts "What God did for us daily in the Sinai, He will do for us in the promised land. He will be our victory, He will be our sustenance."

Gone was the reticence of the first encounter with the Jordan, now they cried with a single faithful voice *"All that thou commandest us we will do, and whithersoever thou sendest us, we will go."* (Josh 1:16)

And so they bowed their heads as one man in humble acceptance. It would not be by their own power that they would conquer in this new land, but by complete submission to God.

And so, on the cliff, one by one the members of the small band lifted their feet from the last support offered by the ledge, and hung fully surrendered from the cord. And they entered in. The death to self was completed in the harsh lands, and they were free now to enter into the rest that God had promised.

And so the ark was carried forward into the Jordan, the pillar of smoke above it to indicate God's unending presence. Into the water the priests went and God stopped the Jordan so that the people might pass by. God in the midst of the water, and the people passing by on either side. They lay the last of their trepidation and fear into God's care, and it tore from them the last vestige of self.

"God holds the cord. We need not fear."

Across the Jordan

This is the place where the tyrannical rule of the self dies. The first deliverance was from the oppression of the foreign master who ruled us from without. The second deliverance is from the the master who rules us from within.

This is a path of two crosses. On the first cross hangs the Christ, and it bridges that impossible gap that existed between God and man since Eden. On the second hangs the Self, that barred God from the heart of man, and from His rightful enthronement within us.

"And he that taketh not his cross, and followeth after me, is not worthy of me. He that findeth his life shall lose it: and he that loseth his life for my sake shall find it"(Mat 10:38,39)

Stage 3: The Promised Land

In the midst of the river, and then again upon the shore, Joshua urges the men of Israel to build a pillar of stones in order that we remember what happened here. And so the metaphor comes to an end, like the "Impressive Dream" of Mrs. White which closes as they touch their feet to the sweet grass.

But what is this place?

Reborn into a new life, wholly and completely surrendered to God, and that empty vessel now receives the greatest gift of God - the filling of the Holy Spirit.

It is from here that we will teach the gospel of what Christ did in us. For what gospel could we teach when we were tormented by the self that yet lived in us? It is here that we can lay our hands upon the fullness of the promises.

Why else would He give us the greatest of these promises except as He desired us to receive them? And what an evil of current thought and theology that we would deny ourselves and others these things by making them unobtainable now - but rather a gift of the far future, or the domain of some special few. Every promise of the Word is yours to grasp hold of, every truth yours to experience.

The third stage is the difference between our God by our side, and our God within us. In John 14:17, Christ says that the Spirit *"dwelleth WITH you"* and then adds that in the near future that He *"shall be IN you."* What a promise! God Himself working

Across the Jordan

out His Word within us!

Why would we settle for small common lives such as Satan and Self would have us live - lives in which the Spirit of God is forced to stand outside and knock, when the very fullness and power of that Divine Life is offered to live itself out within us? I do not suggest that we become great, but that in the very act of becoming small, we allow God to become great in us.

There is no room for pride here, but the outworking of the plan of salvation in man as God had intended. Did not Paul say "I do not live" before he said that "God lives in me"? For before God can work, will, and to do of His good pleasure within us, we must be sacrificed, and the very essence of ourselves killed upon the proffered cross. We die with Him, that He might be raised in us.

No Biblical analogy is so powerful as the one that Christ spoke to Nicodemus, *"Verily, verily, I say unto thee, Except a man be born again, he cannot see the kingdom of God."* (John 3:3) To be reborn, we must of necessity die. And to die with Christ, is to live again by His power. What greater metaphor did we require? There is no half measure here, no "try to be nice and you will see the kingdom of God" there is no "day by day I will make you a better person until one day you will see the kingdom of God." Not but complete destruction of self is required to experience the complete gift of God. God does not repair us, He replaces us.

Christ went on to say that we must be born of water - the Red Sea experience in which we passed from our old life into the preparation time - and "born of the Spirit" in which we graduate from our preparation and receive the Spirit of God within us.

Verily, verily, I say unto thee, Except a man be born of water and [of] the Spirit, he cannot enter into the kingdom of God.
(John 3:5)

"For John truly baptized with water; but ye shall be baptized

with the Holy Ghost not many days hence." (Acts 1:5)

We were baptised by John's baptism, the first baptism into repentance as separation from the world, from Egypt. But there yet remains a baptism.

Philip's good work in Samaria had created a host of new converts, but it wasn't until Peter and John came to help that the missing element to the converts lives could be added:

"Who, when they were come down, prayed for them, that they might receive the Holy Ghost: For as yet he was fallen upon none of them: only they were baptized in the name of the Lord Jesus. Then laid they their hands on them, and they received the Holy Ghost." (Acts: 8:14-16)

"Only" were they baptized. The NASB translates it this way: *"For He had not yet fallen upon any of them; they had simply been baptized in the name of the Lord Jesus."*

Thayer suggests that the greek word here defined "simply" is synonymous with "merely". They were "merely" baptized, they had not yet received the promise. They had merely begun their journey, merely been called.

When speaking metaphorically of the Israelites at the border of the Promised Land, Paul states: *"There remaineth therefore a rest to the people of God. For he that is entered into his rest, he also hath ceased from his own works, as God did from his. Let us labour therefore to enter into that rest, lest any man fall after the same example of unbelief."* (Heb 4:9-11) Some have interpreted this "rest" to mean death. But we require no step of faith to enter into death, and no lack of faith will keep us from dying.

But the Jordan is a kind of death, the death that results in the new birth. And that Promised Land, that "green field", is our place of new birth.

Across the Jordan

What God did, He did in two transitions: He brought us out of Egypt, stage one, and He brought us into Canaan, stage 2. *"And he brought us out from thence, that he might bring us in, to give us the land which he sware unto our fathers."* (Deut 6:2)

The purpose of the first was to accomplish the second. God brought us out of the land of Egypt, in order to bring us into the land of promise. *"Let us therefore fear, lest, a promise being left us of entering into his rest, any of you should seem to come short of it."*

Conclusion

Twelve men wandered the desert with only one baptism when Paul encountered them "*He said unto them, Have ye received the Holy Ghost since ye believed? And they said unto him, We have not so much as heard whether there be any Holy Ghost.*" Paul did not speak of some vague promptings of their consciences when he spoke of the Spirit, but of the power of God himself that longs to live in us. And he could ask, and expect an answer "*Have ye received the Holy Ghost?*"

And might not Paul, if he walked the earth today, ask the same question of us? And might not we say with these twelve "We never heard that there was to be any receiving of the Spirit, we looked around us at all the other disciples of John, recipients of John's baptism, and saw no requirement for anything else!"

We, like those twelve, have wandered with but a single baptism for "*John verily baptized with the baptism of repentance*". But there is something more than the first repentance, there is something more than heeding the initial call of Christ. For to heed that call is to cross the Red Sea, but there is a journey yet to make.

There is a new land beyond the wilderness that God calls us to. And we can enter into that land with these twelve: "*And when Paul had laid [his] hands upon them, the Holy Ghost came on them; and they spake with tongues, and prophesied.*" (Acts 19:6)

Open the word again, and read there the promise that God wills you to journey *through* the land of pain and desolation into the land of plenty.

Across the Jordan

We were never meant to reside here, this was never meant to be our home.

And from the new land we can become the effective messengers with power to those who still live in Egypt. For what resident amongst the apparent wealth of Egypt would welcome the call to go live in the desert?

The dwellers of this land have become as dry and desolate as the place they have pitched their tents. The "good news" that is the gospel is the gift of the promised land, just as the gift was promised to God's children while they yet lived in Egypt. And with Caleb we might say *"Let us go up at once, and possess it; for we are well able to overcome it."* (Numbers 13:30)

For this next chart, I will attempt to reassign the terms that were displaced by adding the third stage. There are also new terms here that have not been touched upon. Let this be fuel to your own study of the word. Be as the Bereans, for they "searched the scriptures daily, whether those things were so."

REDEFINING THE STAGES

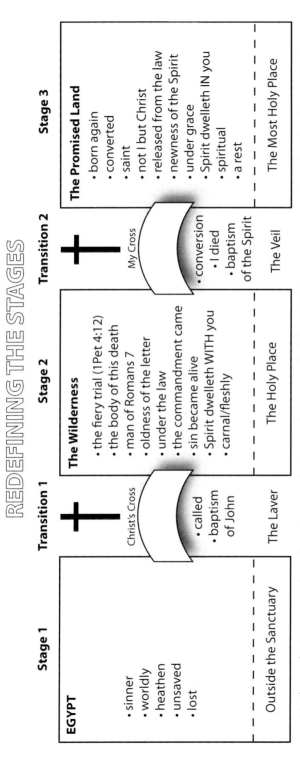

Stage 1	Transition 1	Stage 2	Transition 2	Stage 3
EGYPT	Christ's Cross	**The Wilderness**	My Cross	**The Promised Land**
• sinner • worldly • heathen • unsaved • lost	• called • baptism of John	• the fiery trial (1Pet 4:12) • the body of this death • man of Romans 7 • oldness of the letter • under the law • the commandment came • sin became alive • Spirit dwelleth WITH you • carnal/fleshly	• conversion • I died • baptism of the Spirit	• born again • converted • saint • not I but Christ • released from the law • newness of the Spirit • under grace • Spirit dwelleth IN you • spiritual • a rest
Outside the Sanctuary	The Laver	The Holy Place	The Veil	The Most Holy Place

Verily, verily, I say unto thee, Except a man be born of water and of the Spirit, he cannot enter into the kingdom of God. That which is born of the flesh is flesh; and that which is born of the Spirit is spirit. - John 3:6

29

Across the Jordan

A Prayer for the Path

"O Lord, I will that you reveal my selfish nature to me
so that I might know that there is no good in me.

I pray that you guide me up the path of humility each day.
Let not one day go by that you do not teach my foot to move
forward. Take from me each day some portion of my pride and
my self reliance.

And each time I feel the pain of the loss of that self, each time
I feel the tearing in my soul, let me look to you Lord and say
'Thank you for this gift.'

Let me be humble before all men, and all circumstances that
teach me humility and see them all as being portions of that
heavenly gift of death to self.

Place my flesh upon the offered cross, let it die here. Then call
me from the grave, roll back the stone, and raise me up to new
life.

Before me lies the promised land, I will to enter in."

Across the Jordan

APPENDIX 1

An Impressive Dream
E.G. WHITE
1868 - 2T 594

While at Battle Creek in August, 1868, I dreamed of being with a large body of people. A portion of this assembly started out prepared to journey. We had heavily loaded wagons. As we journeyed, the road seemed to ascend. On one side of this road was a deep precipice; on the other was a high, smooth, white wall, like the hard finish upon plastered rooms.

As we journeyed on, the road grew narrower and steeper. In some places it seemed so very narrow that we concluded that we could no longer travel with the loaded wagons. We then loosed them from the horses, took a portion of the luggage from the wagons and placed it upon the horses, and journeyed on horseback. As we progressed, the path still continued to grow narrow. We were obliged to press close to the wall, to save ourselves from falling off the narrow road down the steep precipice. As we did this, the luggage on the horses pressed against the wall and caused us to sway toward the precipice. We feared that we should fall and be dashed in pieces on the rocks. We then cut the luggage from the horses, and it fell over the precipice. We continued on horseback, greatly fearing, as we came to the narrower places in the road, that we should lose our balance and fall. At such times a hand seemed to take the bridle and guide us over the perilous way.

Across the Jordan

As the path grew more narrow, we decided that we could no longer go with safety on horseback, and we left the horses and went on foot, in single file, one following in the footsteps of another. At this point small cords were let down from the top of the pure white wall; these we eagerly grasped, to aid us in keeping our balance upon the path. As we traveled, the cord moved along with us. The path finally became so narrow that we concluded that we could travel more safely without our shoes, so we slipped them from our feet and went on some distance without them. Soon it was decided that we could travel more safely without our stockings; these were removed, and we journeyed on with bare feet.

We then thought of those who had not accustomed themselves to privations and hardships. Where were such now? They were not in the company. At every change some were left behind, and those only remained who had accustomed themselves to endure hardships. The privations of the way only made these more eager to press on to the end.

Our danger of falling from the pathway increased. We pressed close to the white wall, yet could not place our feet fully upon the path, for it was too narrow. We then suspended nearly our whole weight upon the cords, exclaiming: "We have hold from above! We have hold from above!" The same words were uttered by all the company in the narrow pathway. As we heard the sounds of mirth and revelry that seemed to come from the abyss below, we shuddered. We heard the profane oath, the vulgar jest, and low, vile songs. We heard the war song and the dance song. We heard instrumental music and loud laughter, mingled with cursing and cries of anguish and bitter wailing, and were more anxious than ever to keep upon the narrow, difficult pathway. Much of the time we were compelled to suspend our whole weight upon the cords, which increased in size as we progressed.

I noticed that the beautiful white wall was stained with blood. It caused a feeling of regret to see the wall thus stained. This feeling, however, lasted but for a moment, as I soon thought that it was all as it should be. Those who are following after will know that others have passed the narrow, difficult way before them, and will conclude that if others were able to pursue their onward course, they can do the same. And as the blood shall be pressed from their aching feet, they will not faint with discouragement; but, seeing the blood upon the wall, they will know that others have endured the same pain.

At length we came to a large chasm, at which our path ended. There was nothing now to guide the feet, nothing upon which to rest them. Our whole reliance must be upon the cords, which had increased in size until they were as large as our bodies. Here we were for a time thrown into perplexity and distress. We inquired in fearful whispers: "To what is the cord attached?" My husband was just before me. Large drops of sweat were falling from his brow, the veins in his neck and temples were increased to double their usual size, and suppressed, agonizing groans came from his lips. The sweat was dropping from my face, and I felt such anguish as I had never felt before. A fearful struggle was before us. Should we fail here, all the difficulties of our journey had been experienced for nought.

Before us, on the other side of the chasm, was a beautiful field of green grass, about six inches high. I could not see the sun; but bright, soft beams of light, resembling fine gold and silver, were resting upon this field. Nothing I had seen upon earth could compare in beauty and glory with this field. But could we succeed in reaching it? was the anxious inquiry. Should the cord break, we must perish. Again, in whispered anguish, the words were breathed: "What holds the cord?" For a moment we hesitated to venture. Then we exclaimed: "Our only hope is to trust wholly to the cord. It has been our dependence all the difficult way. It will not fail us now." Still we were hesitating and distressed. The words were then spoken: "God holds the cord. We need not fear." These words were then repeated by those behind us, accompanied with: "He will not fail us now. He has brought us thus far in safety."

My husband then swung himself over the fearful abyss into the beautiful field beyond. I immediately followed. And, oh, what a sense of relief and gratitude to God we felt! I heard voices raised in triumphant praise to God. I was happy, perfectly happy.

I awoke, and found that from the anxiety I had experienced in passing over the difficult route, every nerve in my body seemed to be in a tremor. This dream needs no comment. It made such an impression upon my mind that probably every item in it will be vivid before me while my memory shall continue.

A Prayer For Humility
(An excerpt from the Final Chapter of
"Humility" by Andrew Murray)

I will here give you an infallible touchstone, that will try all to the truth. It is this: retire from the world and all conversation, only for one month; neither write, nor read, nor debate anything with yourself; stop all the former workings of your heart and mind: and, with all the strength of your heart, stand all this month, as continually as you can, in the following form of prayer to God.

Offer it frequently on your knees; but whether sitting, walking, or standing, be always inwardly longing, and earnestly praying this one prayer to God:

"That of His great goodness He would make known to you, and take from your heart, every kind and form and degree of Pride, whether it be from evil spirits, or your own corrupt nature; and that He would awaken in you the deepest depth and truth of that Humility, which can make you capable of His light and Holy Spirit."

Reject every thought, but that of waiting and praying in this matter from the bottom of your heart, with such truth and earnestness, as people in torment wish to pray and be delivered from it ...

If you can and will give yourself up in truth and sincerity to this spirit of prayer, I will venture to affirm that, if you had twice as many evil spirits in you as Mary Magdalene had, they will all be cast out of you, and you will be forced with her to weep tears of love at the feet of the holy Jesus.

Further Suggested Reading
(in no specific order)

Humility ....Andrew Murray
Absolute Surrender ....Andrew Murray
Steps to Christ..Ellen G. White
Higher Christian Life ....William Boardman
Addresses to Clergy ....William Law
A Serious Call* ....William Law
Pursuit of God..A.W. Tozer
The Divine Conquest ....A.W. Tozer
How to Live the Victorious Life.............Unknown Christian
A Plain Account of Christian Perfection ....John Wesley
The Practice of the Presence of God........Brother Lawrence

Most of these titles will be made available free of charge
in the coming months on the website:
www.AcrossTheJordan.com
in the resources section.

*John Wesley calls it one of three books which accounted for his first "explicit
resolve to be all devoted to God." Later he added that "Methodists carefully
read these books and were greatly profitted by them." In 1744 he published
extracts from the Serious Call, thereby introducing it to a wider audience than
it already had. About eighteen months before his death, he called it "a treatise
which will hardly be excelled, if it be equalled, either for beauty of expression
or for depth of thought."*